Alison Primrose

At Home With
REASONING SKILLS
Verbal

OXFORD
UNIVERSITY PRESS

Introduction

The *At Home With* workbooks introduce and reinforce key numeracy and literacy concepts for primary school children. They provide lots of opportunities to develop the key skills that are the basis of primary school curriculum work. The workbooks are available in three levels: 3–5 years, 5–7 years, and 7–9 years. The activities are fun and are designed to stimulate discussion, as well as practical skills. Some children will be able to complete the activities alone, after initial discussion; others may benefit from adult support throughout. All children will enjoy rewarding themselves with a sticker when they reach the end of an activity.

Using the book

- The questions, puzzles, and challenges in this book all develop basic skills for being able to tackle verbal reasoning questions. Sometimes questions require you to look carefully at the letters within a word, whereas other questions depend on knowing the meanings of words. For most questions the answer is given at the back of the book. There are a few open questions where there are many possible answers. For these questions one possible solution is suggested at the back.
- Each double page has a common thematic context, i.e. garden, sports etc.
- Each page is then divided into separate activities.

Helping your child

- Always talk through the work on the page to make sure your child understands what he or she is working on.
- Don't do too much at one sitting. One double page and its test is probably enough at a time for a child's concentration span.
- Most importantly, give plenty of praise and encouragement. Learning always works best when based on success, fun and enjoyment!

OXFORD
UNIVERSITY PRESS

Great Clarendon Street, Oxford OX2 6DP

Oxford University Press is a department of the University of Oxford.
Oxford is a registered trade mark of Oxford University Press
in the UK and in certain other countries

© Oxford University Press 2009

Text copyright © Alison Primrose
Cover illustration by Bill Bolton
Inside illustrations by Bill Bolton

Database right Oxford University Press (maker)

First published in 2009
This edition 2013

British Library Cataloguing in Publication Data

Data available

ISBN: 978 0 19 273428 0

2 4 6 8 10 9 7 5 3

Printed in China

Paper used in the production of this book is a natural,
recyclable product made from wood grown in sustainable forests.
The manufacturing process conforms to the environmental
regulations of the country of origin.

CONTENTS

Page	Topic	similarities/odd one out	analogies	anagrams	word meanings	making new words	selecting words	alphabetical order	crosswords	codes
4	Pond	X	X	X			X			
6	Feelings	X			X	X	X			X
8	Garden	X			X	X			X	
10	Sports	X			X			X	X	
12	Snow	X		X		X				X
14	Rescue	X			X	X			X	
16	Seaside	X	X		X	X				X
18	Castles	X			X			X	X	
20	Picnic	X		X		X			X	
22	Day out	X			X	X				X
24	Bugs	X	X		X					
26	Treasure	X					X	X	X	
28	Party Time	X						X	X	

Pond

Which one belongs?

All the words written in the pond are similar in a special way.
Look carefully to see how they are similar. Then look at the words around the pond – which ones are similar in the same way? Write them in the pond.

❗ Clue: Look carefully at the letters in each word!

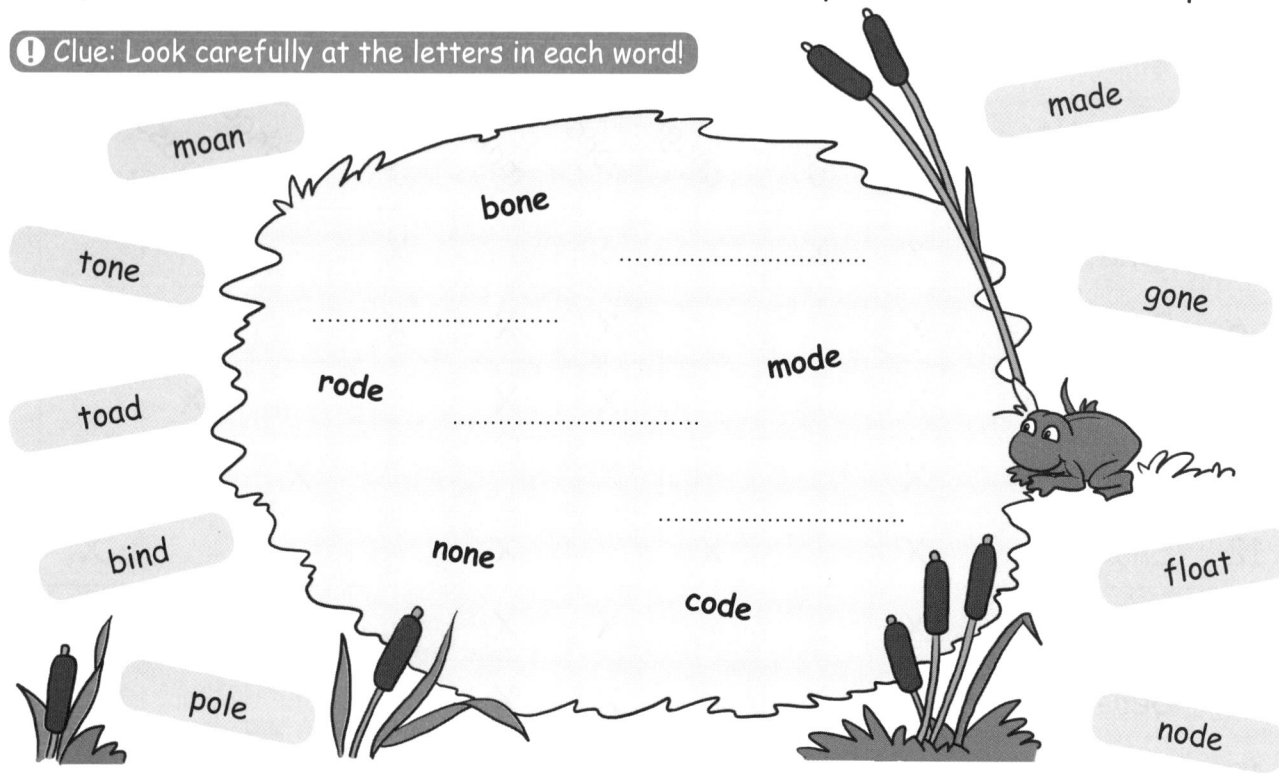

moan

made

bone

tone

gone

mode

rode

toad

bind

float

code

pole

node

Complete these sentences by writing in the correct word.

❗ Hint: Use a dictionary if you are not sure how to spell a word!

1. **Tadpole** is to **frog** as **caterpillar** is to ....

2. **Kitten** is to **cat** as **puppy** is to ....

3. **Bird** is to **air** as **fish** is to...................................... .

4. **Pond** is to **lake** as **stream** is to ....

Pond

In these sentences the letters of some words have been muddled up. Read the sentence to work out what the word should be and then write it with the letters in the correct order. The first one has been done for you.

1. The water snails were eating the (n e e d p o d w) <u>pondweed</u>.

2. The beautiful dragonfly had (l e u b) .... wings.

3. The ducks and (s n a w s) .... were swimming on the pond.

4. The seven (u k n s d c i l g) .... were bright yellow.

5. The children sailed their (t o b a s) .... across the pond.

These sentences describe ponds. In each sentence there is a gap followed by 3 words in brackets. Choose the word from the brackets that best completes the sentence and write it in the gap. The first one has been done for you.

1. The bird's nest was hidden in the tall <u>rushes</u> (building / rushes / gates) near the pond.

2. The bottom of a pond is usually very .... (blue / wet / muddy).

3. The wind makes ripples on the .... (edge / weeds / surface) of the pond.

4. The children caught the fish with their .... (feet / eyes / nets).

5. The lily flowers opened up in the warm .... (sunshine / night / wind).

Feelings

Different words have been used to describe how these children are feeling. Three of the four words are similar – can you circle the odd one out?

1. happy   content   pleased   annoyed

2. gloomy   sad   angry   upset

3. confused   muddled   sad   uncertain

4. content   cross   angry   annoyed

Make FOUR new words from each of the words given on the left, just by changing one letter at a time. The first one has been done for you.

1. G R I N   GRAN   BRAN   BRAG   DRAG

2. C R Y   ....

3. S M I L E   ....

To complete these sentences, choose a word beginning with the letter shown and rhyming with the word in brackets.

1. Bili is sad and t..........................   (cheerful)

2. Tina is very h..........................   (snappy)

3. Jan is in a bad mood, she is c..........................   (boss)

4. Henry is hot and doesn't feel w..........................   (bell)

Some words have more than one meaning. See if you can find a word that has both of the meanings given below. One has been done for you.

1. A small bird with a forked tail. ....swallow.......... To make food go down your throat.

2. A water drop from your eye. .... To rip up a piece of paper.

3. To be angry or bad-tempered. .... To go across something.

a	b	c	d	e	f	g	h	i	j	k	l	m	n	o	p	q	r	s	t	u	v	w	x	y	z
Z	A	B	C	D	E	F	G	H	I	J	K	L	M	N	O	P	Q	R	S	T	U	V	W	X	Y

If the word **run** is written as a special code, it is written as **QTM**. The word **ate** is **ZSD** in the same code.

Fill in the rest of the code in the squares below the alphabet. Now, decode the following question and challenge.

G N V   Z Q D   X N T   E D D K H M F   S N C Z X ?

h o w   ___ ___ ___   ___ ___ ___   ___ ___ ___ ___ ___ ___ ___   ___ ___ ___ ___ ___ ?

V Q H S D   X N T Q   Z M R V D Q R   H M   B N C D !

___ ___ ___ ___ ___   ___ ___ ___ ___   ___ ___ ___ ___ ___ ___ ___   ___ ___   ___ ___ ___ ___ !

Make up your own code and write a secret message for someone else to decode. How is the word **run** written in your special code? **r u n** ___ ___ ___

a	b	c	d	e	f	g	h	i	j	k	l	m	n	o	p	q	r	s	t	u	v	w	x	y	z

....

....

Garden

Look carefully at these sets of words. In each set, all the words include a particular letter – except one. See if you can circle the word that does not include that letter – it is the odd one out! The first one has been done for you.

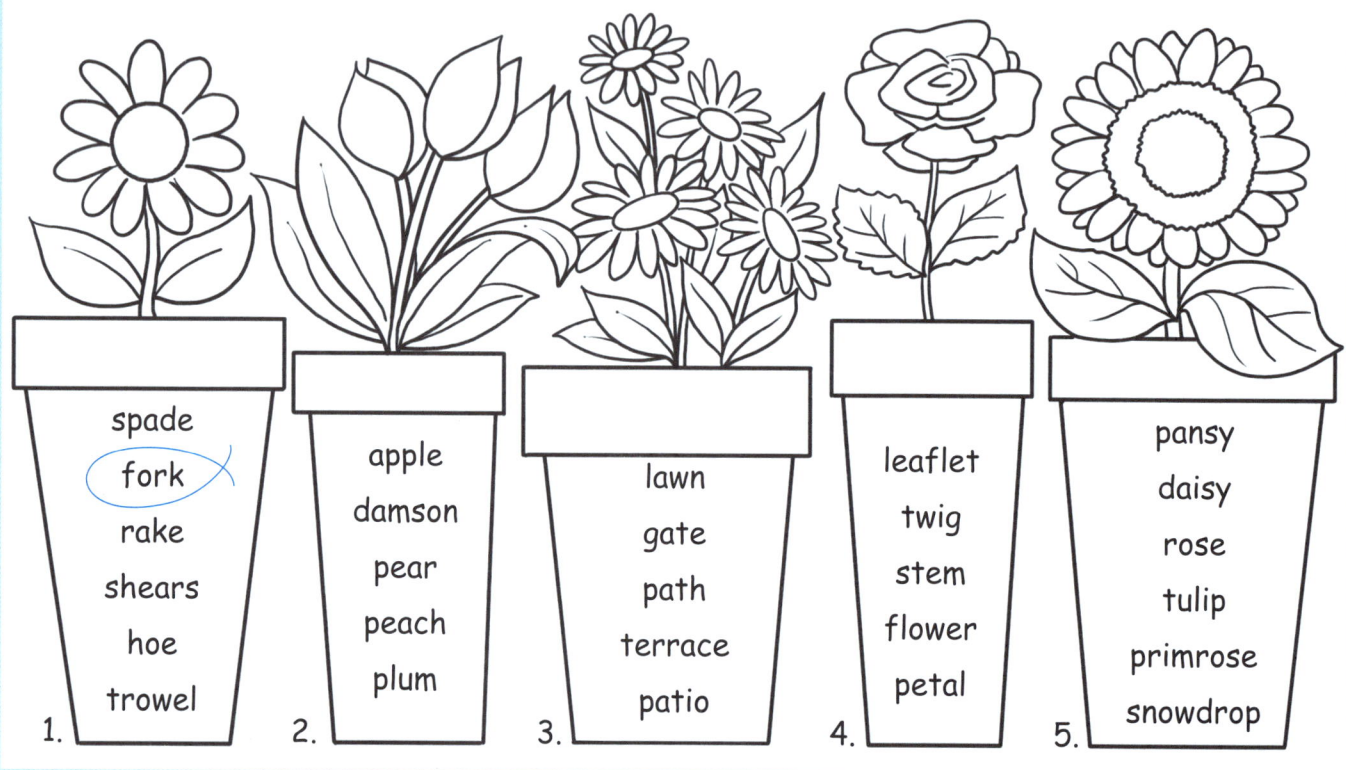

1.
spade
fork
rake
shears
hoe
trowel

2.
apple
damson
pear
peach
plum

3.
lawn
gate
path
terrace
patio

4.
leaflet
twig
stem
flower
petal

5.
pansy
daisy
rose
tulip
primrose
snowdrop

Some words are made up of two words joined together. These are called compound words. Read these sentences and complete them by filling in the missing compound word.

1. It was hot in the _g _ _ _ _ h _ _ _ _ _.

2. He watered the plants in the garden using a _h _ _ _ _ p _ _ _ _.

3. She cut the grass with an electric _l _ _ _ m _ _ _ _ _.

Garden

Complete the grid by writing in the words below.
Make sure they fit with the letters already given.
The word in the blue squares is the name of
a flower – what is it?

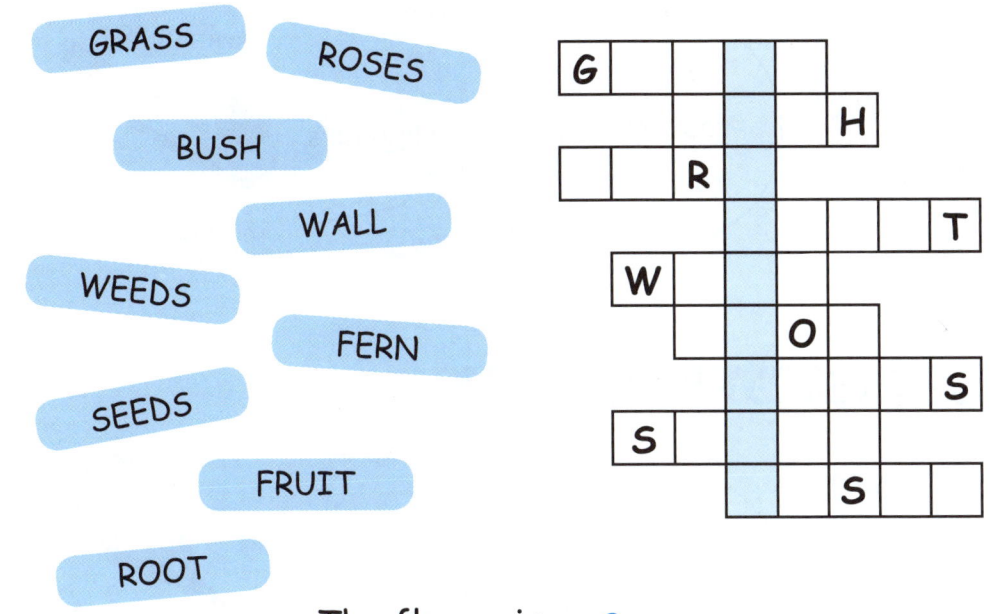

GRASS   ROSES

BUSH

WALL

WEEDS

FERN

SEEDS

FRUIT

ROOT

The flower is a _S_ _ _ _ _ _ _ _ _ _ .

In the following groups of words, two words have very
similar meanings. Circle the two words in each group.
The first one has been done for you.

1. shrub   (flower)   bouquet   (bloom)   colour

2. sharp   thorn   smooth   prickle   wood

3. stem   stalk   trunk   leaf   branch

4. lemon   ruby   emerald   colour   scarlet

5. perfume   manure   scent   roses   special

Sports

Which 4 sports outside the circle belong with the sports inside the circle?
One has been done for you.

1. ❗ Clue: Look carefully at how each sport is spelled.

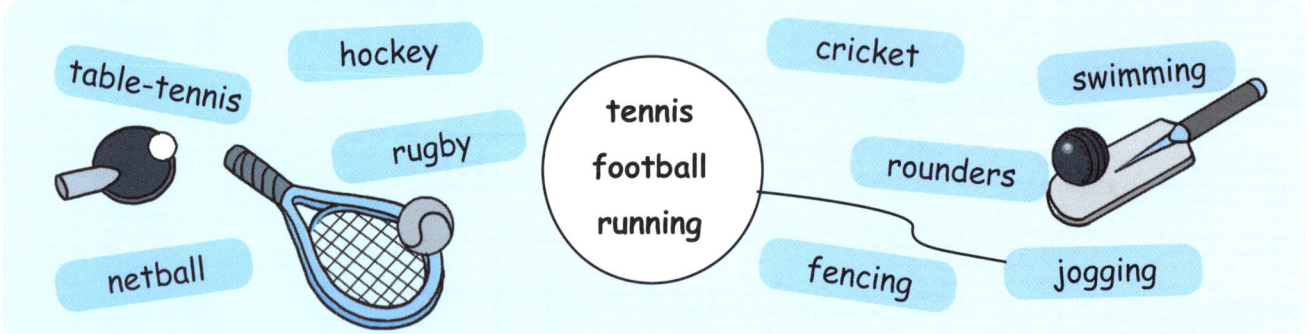

table-tennis
hockey
rugby
netball

cricket
swimming
rounders
fencing
jogging

tennis
football
running

2. ❗ Clue: Now think about each sport and the equipment used.

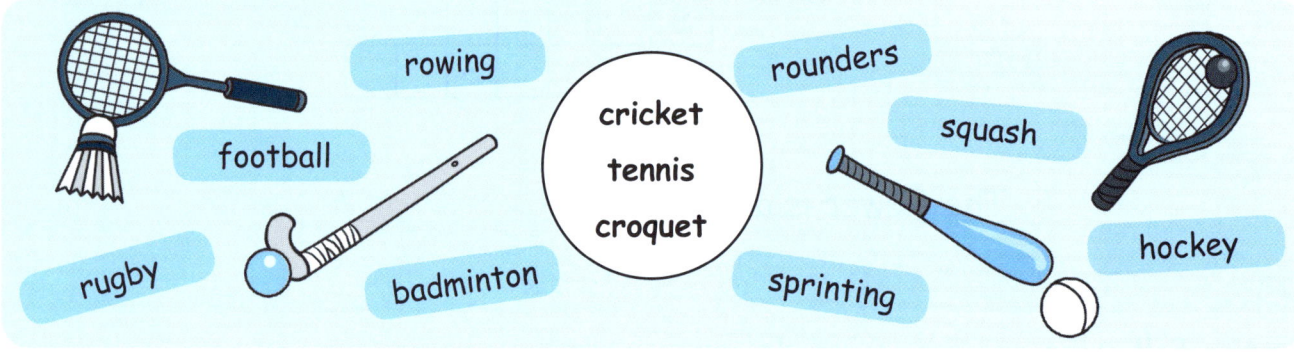

rowing
football
rugby
badminton

rounders
squash
hockey
sprinting

cricket
tennis
croquet

a b c d e f g h i j k l m n o p q r s t u v w x y z

These sports are listed in alphabetical order.

archery   badminton   cricket   rounders   squash   tennis

Put the sports below into alphabetical order. Look carefully at the first letter.
The first one has been started for you.

1. hockey   fencing   golf ⟶ fencing ....

2. curling   badminton   discus ⟶ ....

3. high jump   trampolining   cricket ⟶ ....

4. rowing   judo   karate ⟶ ....

Sports

To be the best, a champion might be the fastest, the strongest, the quickest or go the furthest. They have to be the best.

Read these sentences and then change the word in **bold** type so that the sentence means the complete opposite. Write the new word in the space provided.

1. She was the **slowest**. ....

2. His throw was **closest**. ....

3. She was **last**. ....

4. His jump was **lowest**. ....

Write the sports below in the grid using the letters given already to help you. Find the word hidden in the blue squares.

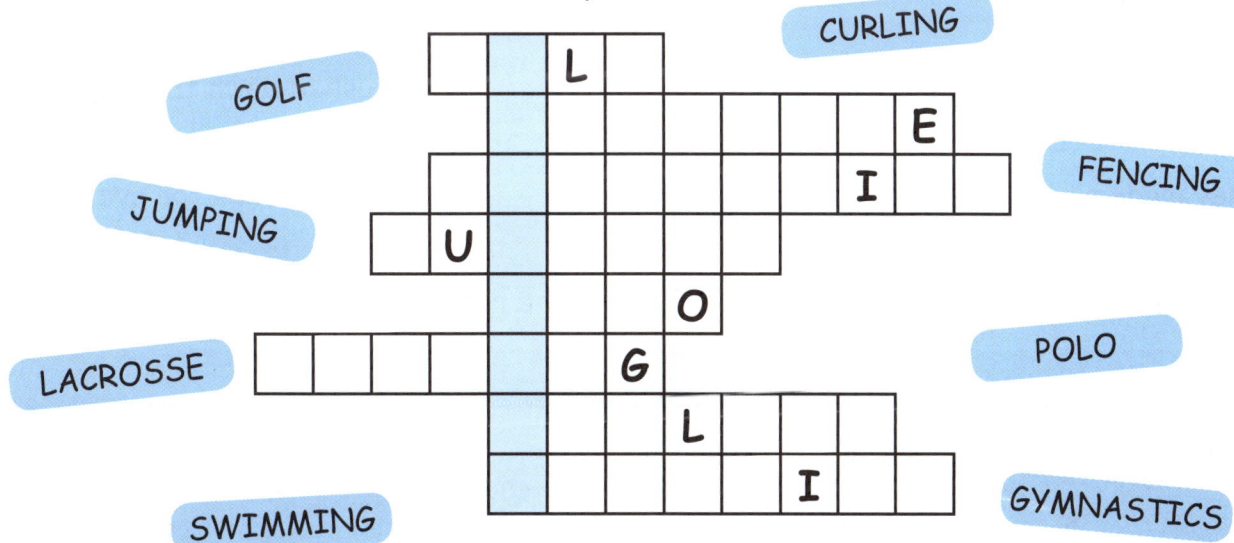

CURLING
GOLF
JUMPING
FENCING
LACROSSE
POLO
SWIMMING
GYMNASTICS

The hidden word is O _ _ _ _ _ _ _ _ .

Snow

1. Circle the odd one out in this set of words. Look carefully at the letters.

notice   rice   recipe

                          entice

slice   police

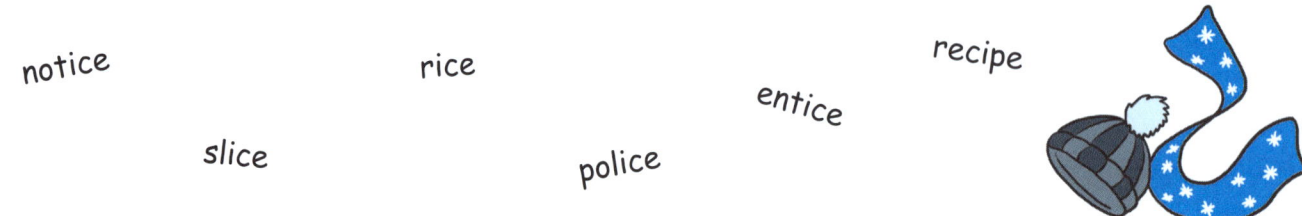

2. Circle the odd one out in this set of words. Think carefully about the word meanings.

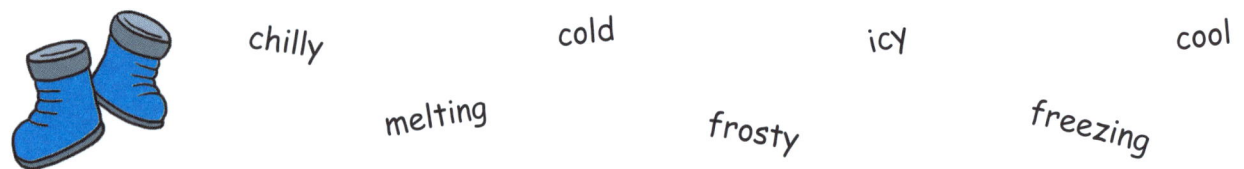

chilly   cold   icy   cool

melting   frosty   freezing

Unscramble the letters in brackets to make a proper word that will complete these sentences sensibly.

1. They all went (g a s k n i t) .... on the frozen lake.

2. The dog chased the (g o b a n g o t) .... as it rushed down the hill!

3. They made a very splendid (n a n w o m s) .... with stones for eyes.

4. The (c l i e c i s) .... along the roof edge melted slowly in the sun.

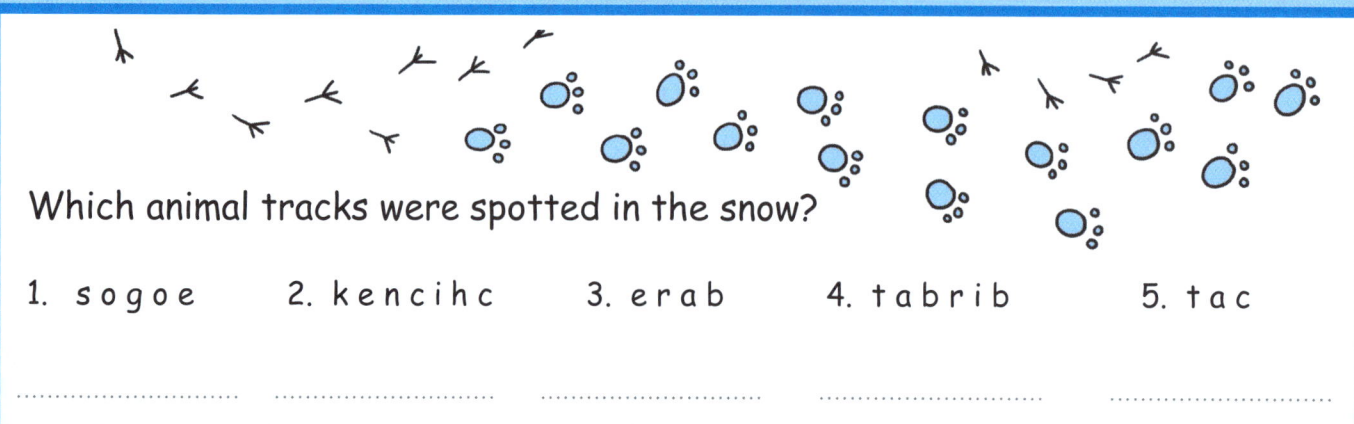

Which animal tracks were spotted in the snow?

1. s o g o e   2. k e n c i h c   3. e r a b   4. t a b r i b   5. t a c

....

Snow

a	b	c	d	e	f	g	h	i	j	k	l	m	n	o	p	q	r	s	t	u	v	w	x	y	z
				d			h						m				q	s				v			

If the code for **winter** is **vhmsdq**, what is the code for **s u m m e r** ?

What do these codes stand for?

_ _ _ _ _ _

1) **r g n d r**

_ _ _ _ _

3) **a z k k r**

_ _ _ _ _

5) **c q n o**

_ _ _ _

7) **b z o**

_ _ _

2) **e k z j d**

_ _ _ _ _

4) **l z m**

_ _ _

6) **e h d k c**

_ _ _ _ _

The words above can all form compound words by being added to the word **snow**, e.g. snowman.

Choose the correct compound word to complete these sentences:

1. They had fun throwing .... at each other.

2. The .... slowly melted in the sun.

3. Their .... stopped them from sinking into the deep snow.

4. Each .... is a beautiful crystal.

Rescue

Each word in the circle belongs to a group below.
Draw a line from each word to link it to the correct group.
The first one has been done for you.

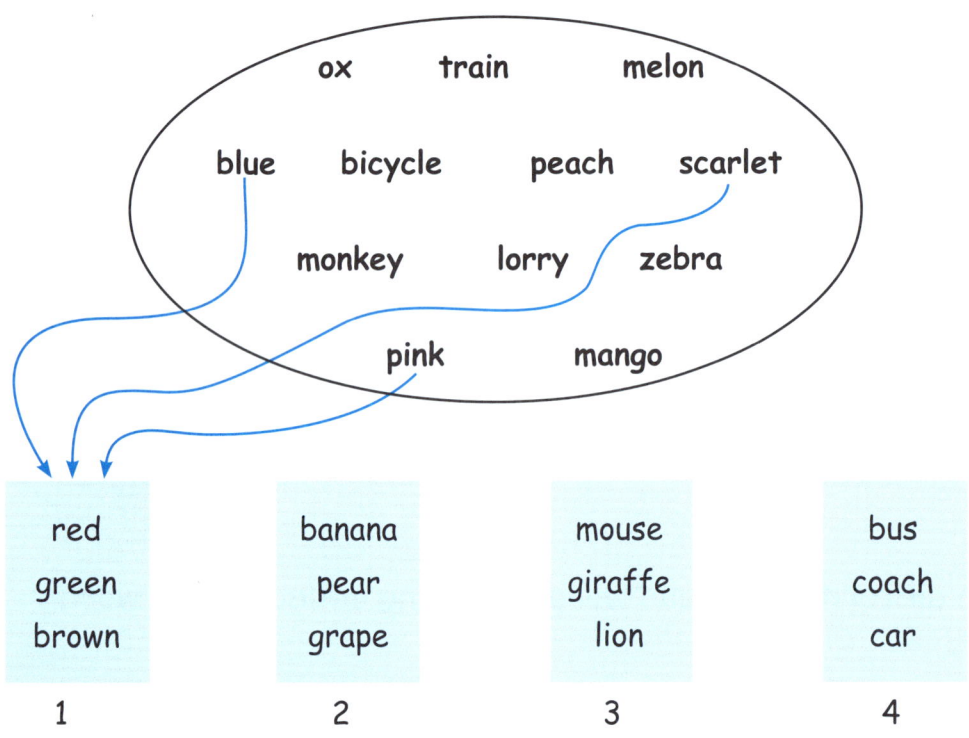

1	2	3	4
red	banana	mouse	bus
green	pear	giraffe	coach
brown	grape	lion	car

Complete these word ladders. Starting at the bottom, change one letter at a time to make a new word, ending with the word given at the top of the ladder. The first one has been done for you.

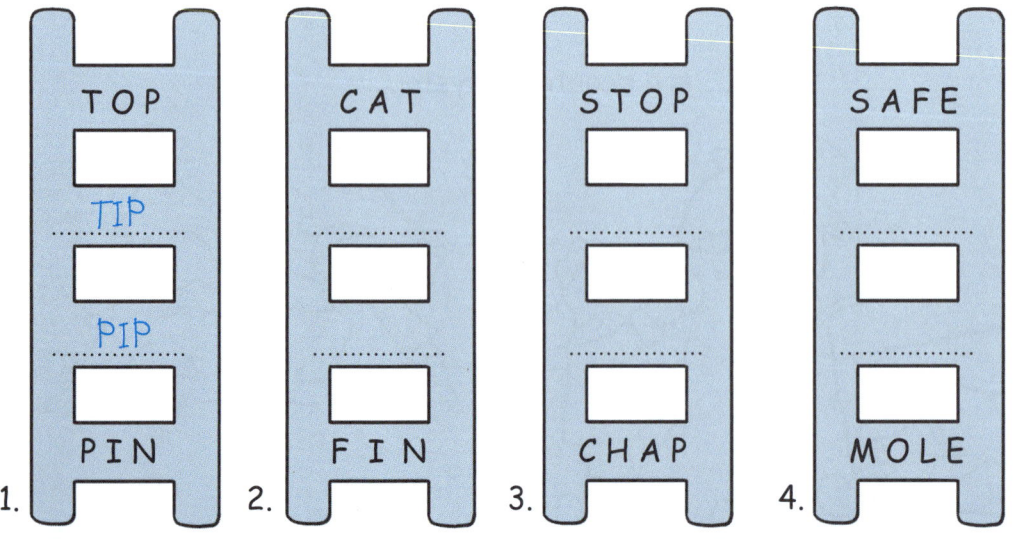

1. TOP / ___ / TIP / ___ / PIP / ___ / PIN

2. CAT / ___ / ___ / ___ / FIN

3. STOP / ___ / ___ / ___ / CHAP

4. SAFE / ___ / ___ / ___ / MOLE

Rescue

Look at this set of three words. Complete the sets in the same way.

	tall		taller		tallest
1.	high	→	....	→	highest
2.	....	→	shorter	→	shortest
3.	low	→	lower	→	....
4.	wide	→	....	→	widest

Some words have more than one meaning. Read both definitions and see if you can write the missing word in the middle. The first one has been done for you.

1. to go pale and fall down ....*faint*............ a faded or dim colour

2. an annoying insect .... to travel in a plane

3. feeling fit and healthy .... a deep water hole

4. part of the body .... a special box for treasure

Look at these words. Write them into the grid using the letters already given. Find the word hidden in the blue squares.

panic   smoke   rescue

ladder   flames

siren

ring   emergency

nine nine nine   quickly

F _ _ _   _ _ _ _ _ _

Seaside

Which words belong in which bucket? The first one has been done for you.

shells

limpets

1.

food

2.

drink

3.

limpets

sandwiches

cola

frisbee

apple

cap

bikini

mussels

bat and ball

t-shirt

squash

sandals

biscuits

water

toys

4.

clothes

5.

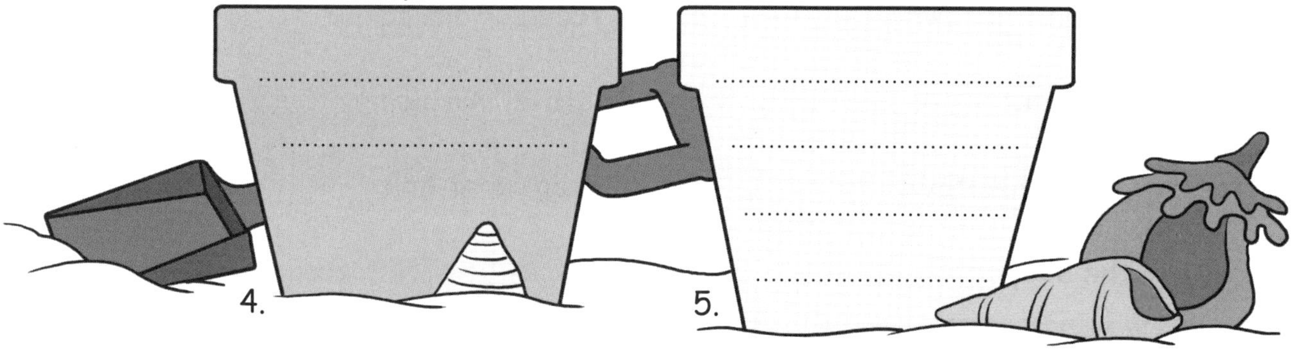

Knife and fork go together – complete these other pairs of things that often go together.

1. salt and ....

2. Punch and ....

3. bucket and ....

4. fish and ....

16

Seaside

Which two words on each kite are most similar in meaning?
Underline them. The first one has been done for you.

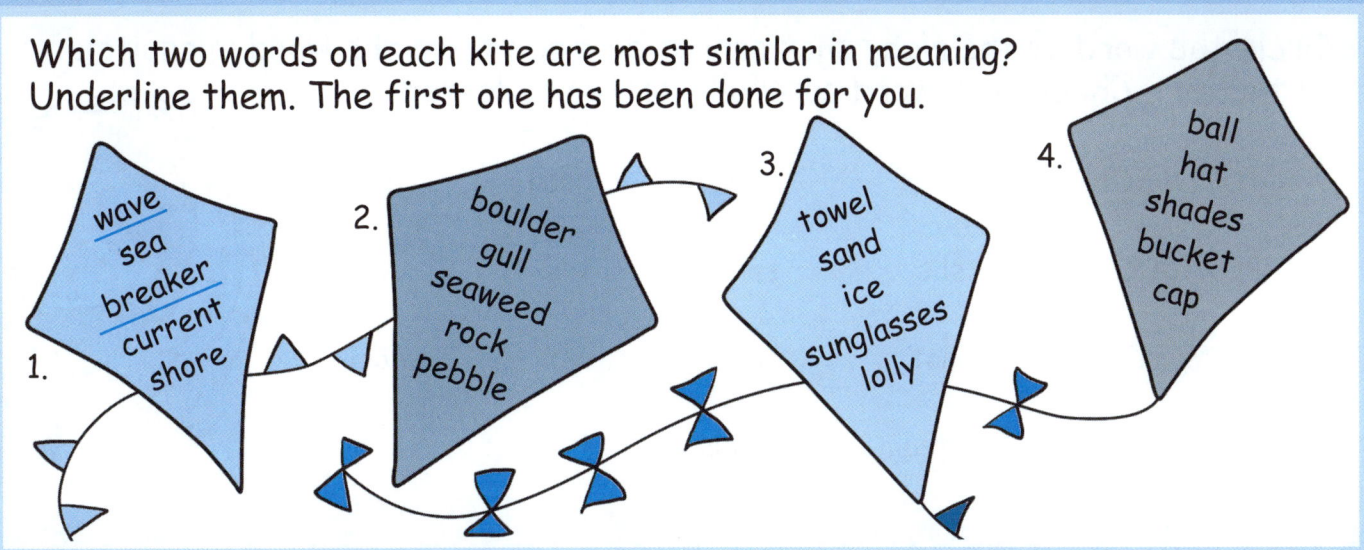

1. wave / sea / breaker / current / shore

2. boulder / gull / seaweed / rock / pebble

3. towel / sand / ice / sunglasses / lolly

4. ball / hat / shades / bucket / cap

Join these words to make new compound words (each word can only be used once).

sea   after   sand   rock

castle   pool   noon   side

1. ....   3. ....

2. ....   4. ....

Children write messages in code to each other when playing on the beach.
Use the code breaker below to work out what the message is.

a	b	c	d	e	f	g	h	i	j	k	l	m	n	o	p	q	r	s	t	u	v	w	x	y	z
♋	♌	♍	♎	♏	♐	♑	♒	♓	er	&	●	○	■	□	□	□	□	•	◆	◆	❖	•	⊠	⌂	⌘

◆♏   ❖♋❖♏   •□○♏   ♍❖□♍□●♋◆♏   ◆□   •❖♋□♏,

<u>w e</u>   _ _ _ _   _ _ _ _   _ _ _ _ _ _ _ _ _   _ _   _ _ _ _ _,

♍□○♏   ♋●□■♑   ◆□   ◆❖♏   ♍♋❖♏.

_ _ _ _   _ _ _ _ _   _ _   _ _ _   _ _ _ _.

17

Castles

Circle the word on the right that cannot be made from the word in capitals on the left. Check each word carefully, letter by letter.

1. DUNGEON   done   neon   gong   node

2. PORTCULLIS   slit   spill   trip   slice

3. MOAT   mat   toe   oat   tom

4. BATTLEMENTS   steam   meals   title   beast

Medieval castles had many interesting features. See if you can write out this list of features in alphabetical order. If two words have the same first letter, you need to look at the second letter and so on.
The first two have been done for you.

a b c d e f g h i j k l m n o p q r s t u v w x y z

1. archers
2. arrow slits
3. ....
4. ....
5. ....
6. ....
7. ....
8. ....
9. ....
10. ....

archers

keep

arrow slits

battlements

bailey

well

portcullis

gatehouse

horseman

moat

18

Castles

Circle the word on the right that is the opposite of the word in capital letters in the sentence on the left.

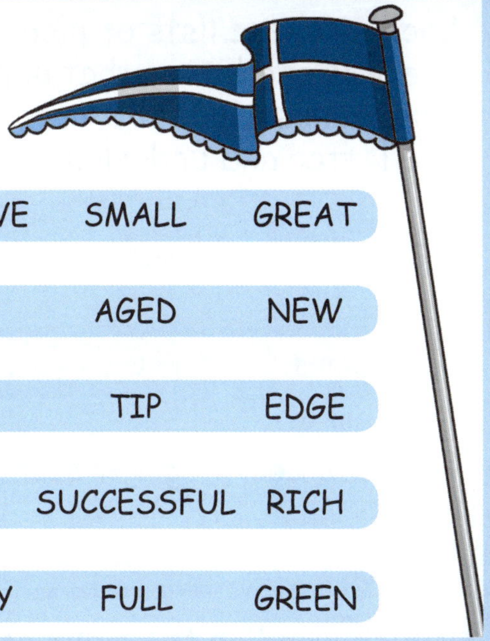

1. The castle was built using LARGE stones.   MASSIVE   SMALL   GREAT

2. It was a very ANCIENT building.   OLD   AGED   NEW

3. The castle was built at the TOP of a hill.   BASE   TIP   EDGE

4. The owner of the castle was very POOR.   KIND   SUCCESSFUL   RICH

5. The moat was EMPTY.   MUDDY   FULL   GREEN

Complete the grids by writing in these words.
Use the letters already in the grid to help you.

TON   TOP

PET   NET

	O	
O	N	E
	E	

BEAST   TIERS

APPLE   AMPLE

TREES   BOAST

Picnic

Look at these lists of picnic foods. In each list, there is one letter that appears in three of the four words. Spot the word which does not include the letter and underline it.

1. egg   ham   cheese   pate

2. apples   pears   bananas   grapes

3. lemonade   ginger beer   coca cola   juice

Which word on the right cannot be made using the letters from the word in capitals on the left? Underline it.

1. SANDWICH   wand   ship   chin   wish

2. SAUSAGES   sages   guess   gauge   gases

3. CHOCOLATE   coal   heat   oath   tell

4. LEMONADE   meal   loan   maid   dame

Unjumble the letters to make words which complete this story sensibly.

One hot, (nunsy) .... day the children went to the (rakp) ....

They wanted to play (toblaflo) .... and to play on the

(gisnws) .... The (odg) .... called Bonjo went with them.

Picnic

Change the blue letter in each of these words to discover what was packed inside the picnic basket.

1. GRASSES ....

2. BREAK ....

3. HAT ....

4. CAPES ....

5. DRAPES ....

6. PEAKS ....

7. DOLLS ....

Find a letter to go in the brackets, so that the letter finishes the word on the left and starts a proper word on the right.

⚠ Clue: You can eat all of these things!

1. M E A (.....) U N A

2. M A N G (.....) R A N G E

3. H A (.....) E L O N

4. M U F F I (.....) U T S

5. C H E E S (.....) G G

Complete the crossword by writing the names of nuts below into the correct spaces. Use the letters already in the crossword to help you.

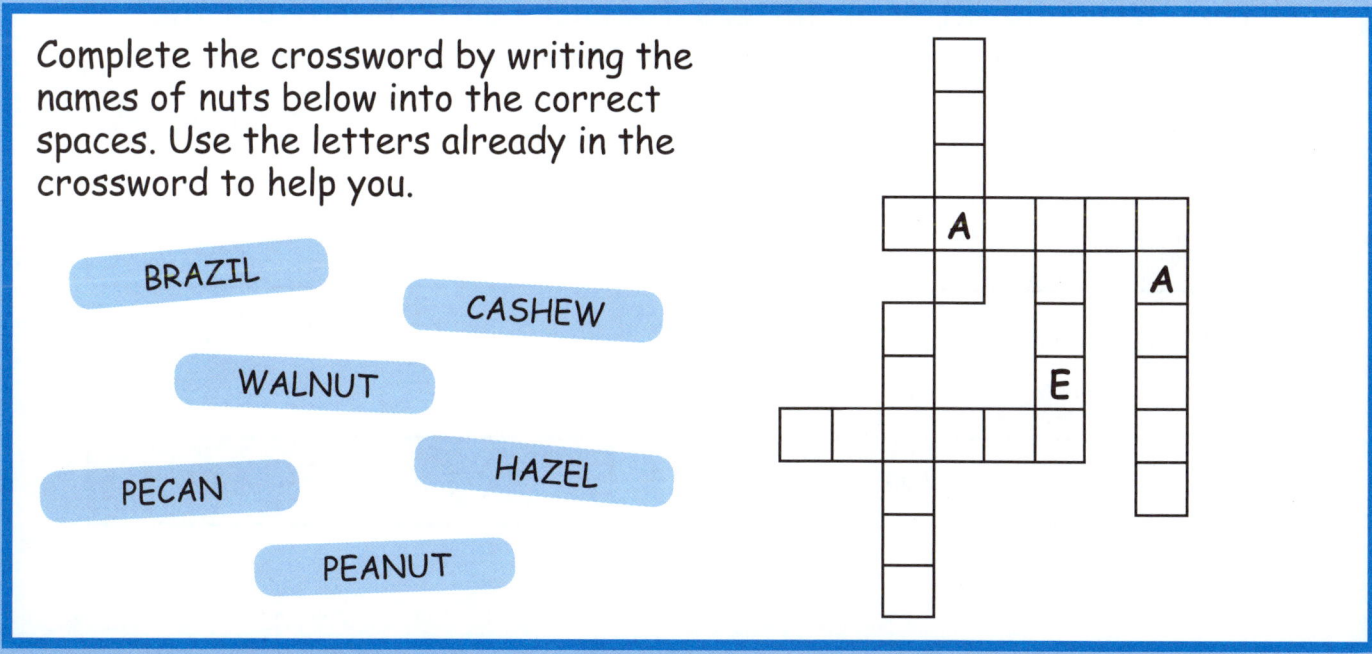

BRAZIL

CASHEW

WALNUT

PECAN

HAZEL

PEANUT

21

Day Out

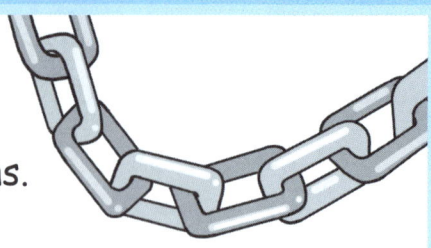

Look carefully at the word chains. There is one pair of letters that occurs in each word in each chain. First find the pair of letters. Then choose 3 words from below to complete the other word chains. The first one has been done for you.

1. T**RA**IN 🔗 **RA**SCAL 🔗 B**RA**IN 🔗 *TRAMP* 🔗 *FORAY* 🔗 *WRAP*

2. COACH 🔗 WINCH 🔗 FRENCH 🔗 ___ 🔗 ___

3. PLANE 🔗 APPLE 🔗 SAMPLE 🔗 ___ 🔗 ___

4. HORSE 🔗 SHOWN 🔗 WHOLE 🔗 ___ 🔗 ___

5. CAR 🔗 CARTON 🔗 SCAR 🔗 ___ 🔗 ___

PLEASE	WHICH	TRAMP	HOTEL	PLENTY
CAMP	FORAY	SUPPLE	WRAP	PECAN
POACH	CHIMP	SHOP	HOUSE	CANAL

The words on these tickets can be made into new words by adding letters before, or after, them. The same letters will make a proper new word for each one. Select the letter, or letters, for each pair and write out the new words. The first one has been done for you.

| ING | RE | DE | F |

1. | LIGHT | ARE |

   FLIGHT   *FARE*

2. | FLY | PARK |

   ___   ___

3. | TURN | PAY |

   ___   ___

4. | PART | LAY |

   ___   ___

Sometimes everything goes wrong! Change the words written in capitals into words that mean the exact opposite to read about the holiday that went wrong . . .

It was a very HOT .... day. There were

SMALL .... WHITE .... clouds

in the sky. It was a SHORT .... journey

in the car. At the hotel they had been given a very

LARGE .... room. The children were

WIDE-AWAKE .... and

NO-ONE .... was hungry.

The family were arranging a surprise day out for Mum. They sent a message to each other in code. Use the clue and the alphabet below to decode the message, then answer the question using the code.

a	b	c	d	e	f	g	h	i	j	k	l	m	n	o	p	q	r	s	t	u	v	w	x	y	z

! Clue: The word **g a r d e n** in code is **i c t f g p**

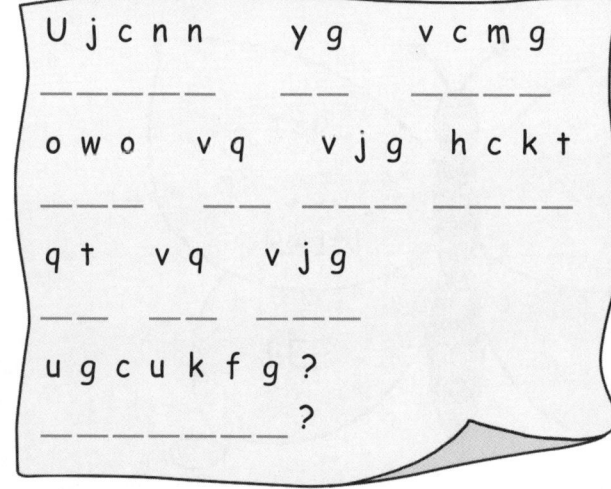

Ujcnn yg vcmg

_ _ _ _ _   _ _   _ _ _ _

owo vq vjg hckt

_ _ _   _ _   _ _ _   _ _ _ _

qt vq vjg

_ _   _ _   _ _ _

ugcukfg?

_ _ _ _ _ _ _ ?

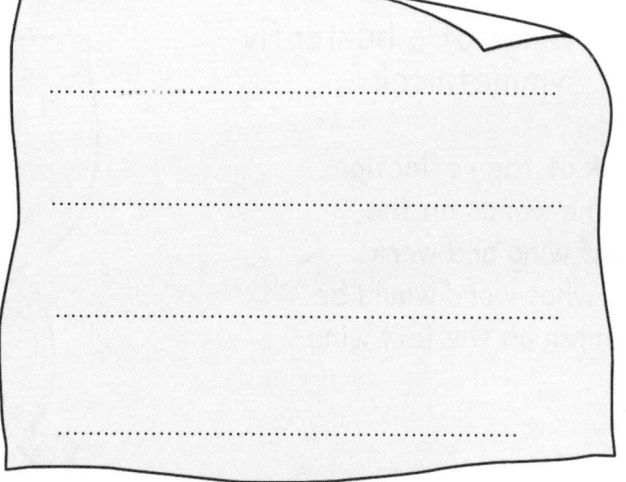

Bugs

In each of these lists, which is the odd one out? Circle it.

! Clue: Look at how the names are spelled.

1.
fly
shy
sky
buy
why
spy

2.
bee
tee
see
knee
fee
wee

3.
beetle
sheet
keel
kettle
meet
between

4.
wasp
rasp
whisper
clasp
jasper
aspirin

Read the first half of each sentence and then select a word to complete the second part of the sentence in the same way as the first part.

1. Humming birds hum and buzzing bees ....

2. Grasshoppers hop and butterflies ....

3. Worms wriggle and snakes ....

4. Spiders run and moths ....

The wings of a butterfly are symmetrical.

Look at the reflection of the words on the right wing and work out what word would be written on the left wing.

24

Bugs

Look at the following lists of words – in each list there are two words that are very similar in meaning. Underline the two most similar words.

1. flying   hovering   spinning   catching   gliding

2. bite   nip   scratch   tickle   rub

3. wriggle   shuffle   slide   waddle   slither

4. buzz   sing   chant   squeak   hum

Look at these groups of minibeasts. Look carefully at their names and circle the odd one out in each group.

❗ Clue: Look at how the names are spelled.

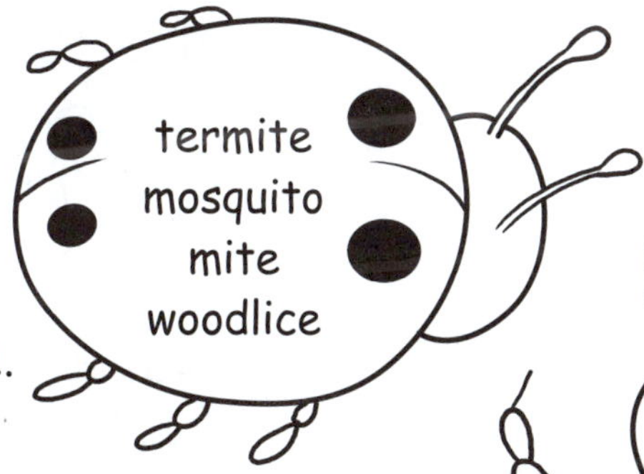

1. termite
mosquito
mite
woodlice

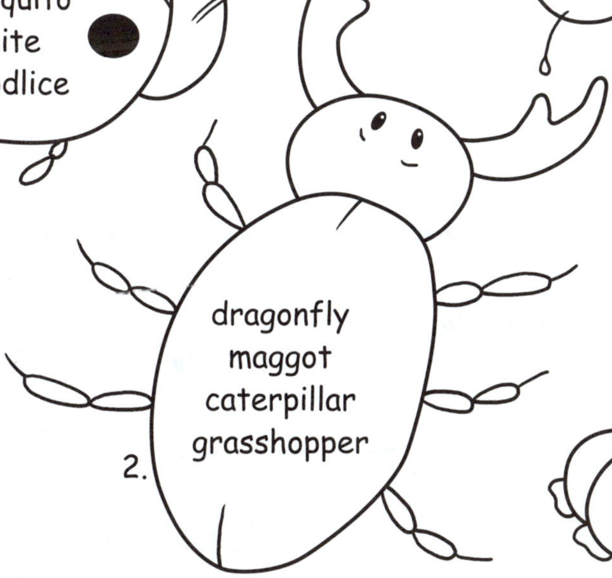

2. dragonfly
maggot
caterpillar
grasshopper

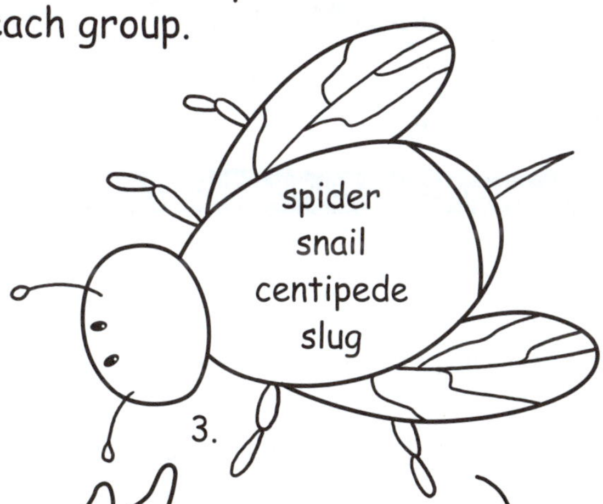

3. spider
snail
centipede
slug

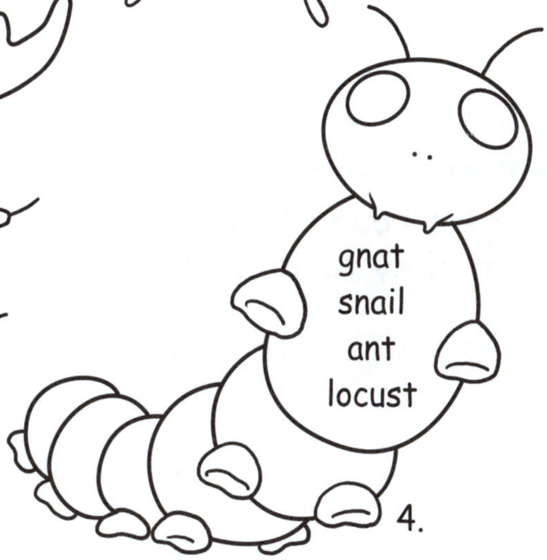

4. gnat
snail
ant
locust

25

Treasure

One letter occurs only once in each of these lists.
Underline the word in which the letter occurs.

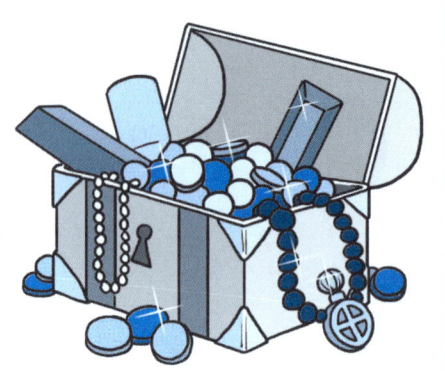

1. gold   lead   glass   goals

2. chest   stone   trove   torch   cover

3. money   loot   golden   mined   gilt

In the following sentences there are some hidden four letter words.
They are made from the second part of one word and the beginning
of the next word.

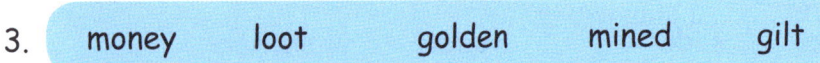

The dame attended the fete. ⟶ meat

See if you can find the four letter words that are hidden in these sentences.

! Clue: All the words are split across a gap, but not always with two letters each side.

1. The jewels were all glittering brightly. ....

2. The children told the pirate to walk the plank! ....

3. One by one they all entered the cave. ....

4. He put the golden lamp into his bag. ....

The pirates found this treasure.
List what they found in alphabetical order.

rings   necklaces
watches   bracelets
clips   bangles

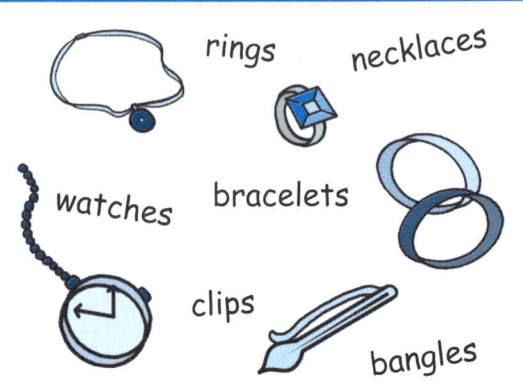

1. ....   4. ....

2. ....   5. ....

3. ....   6. ....

Treasure

Some words have more than one meaning. Look at these pairs of meanings and then choose the word from below that can mean both things.
You will only need 5 of the 10 words given! The first one has been done for you.

1. nasty gas being given off ....fume.......... to be angry

2. a violin .... to play around with something

3. a cool breeze .... fruit straight from the garden

4. a division in the road .... you eat with this

5. to be a quick runner .... to go without food for a time

(fume) fork fancy fry fresh

fine felt fire fiddle fast

Complete this crossword of precious stones and metals.

SILVER

AMBER

OPAL

GOLD

PEARL

EMERALD

AQUAMARINE

GARNET

TURQUOISE

SAPPHIRE

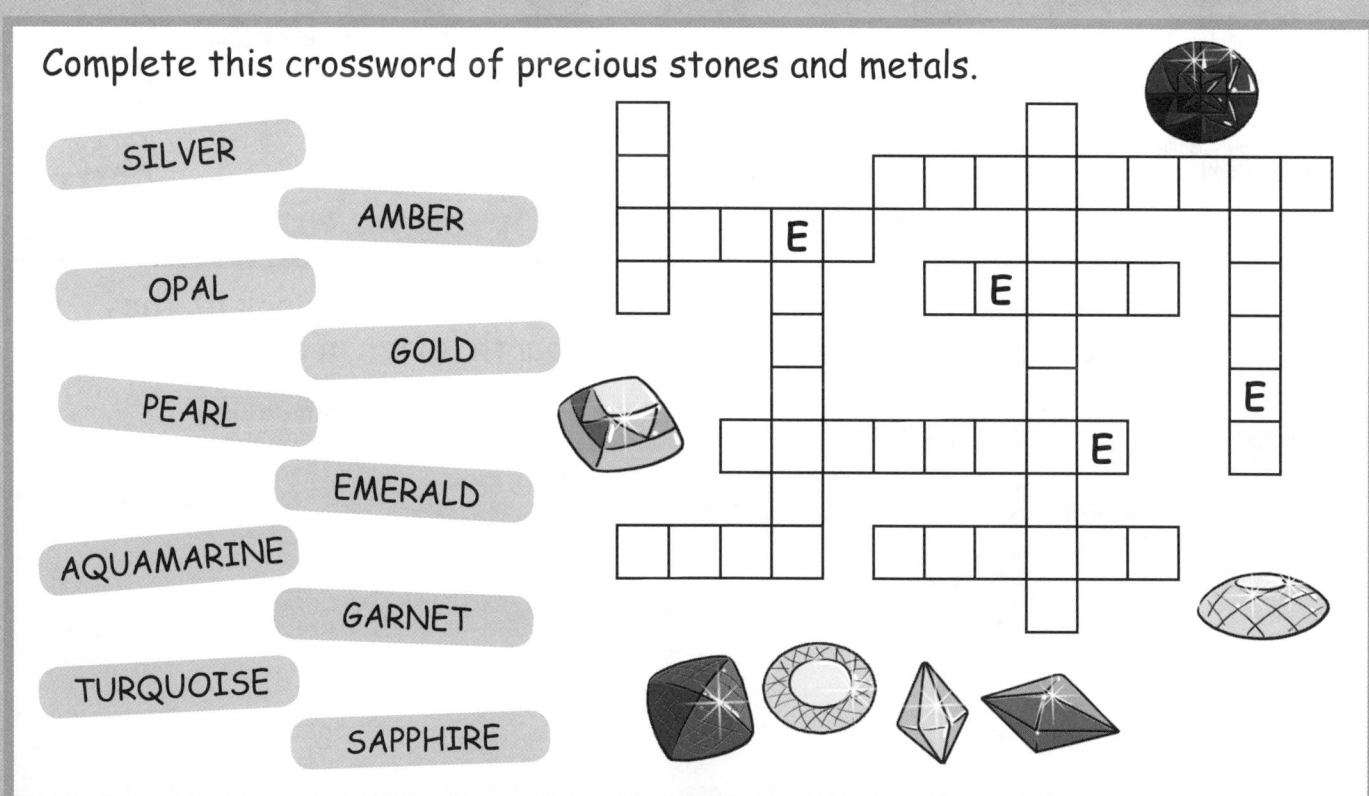

Party Time

Which one is the odd one out in each of these groups? Circle it.
It might be to do with word meanings or spellings so look carefully!

1.   sausage roll   fairy cake   jelly   scotch egg   carrot stick

2.   cookies   chocolate   cheese   muffins   crisps

3.   lemonade   apple   orange   squash   milk   tea

Look at the children who are going to be invited to the party.
Then fill in the names, using the letters already given to help you.

1. _ _ _ _ _   3. _ _ _ _ _   5. _ _ _   7. _ _ _ r _

2. _ _ _ _ o   4. _ _ _ _ _   6. _ _ i _   8. _ _ _ _ _ s

Joe   Lily   Meera   Thomas   Jacob   Ali   Callum   Jacky

Put the names in alphabetical order. They all begin with **A**, so look at the
second letter, and perhaps even the third or fourth letter in each one.

Angela   Abraham   Anna   Amanda

Antony   Alison   Alex   Annie

1. ....   3. ....   5. ....   7. ....

2. ....   4. ....   6. ....   8. ....

Party Time

Look carefully at the following lists. Circle the two words that are most similar in meaning.

1. hat   motto   cup   cracker   cap

2. plate   glass   bowl   cloth   dish

3. frock   trousers   blouse   dress   shorts

4. balloon   streamers   sparklers   paper chain   cracker

Find out what the mystery present is by writing out the word in the blue squares. Look at the presents in the picture and write them into the grid using the letters already given to help you . . .

The mystery present is a

_ _ _ _ .

Answers

Pond

Page 4
top:
1. tone
2. pole
3. gone
4. node

bottom:
1. butterfly
2. dog
3. water
4. river

Page 5
top:
2. blue
3. swans
4. ducklings
5. boats

bottom:
2. muddy
3. surface
4. nets
5. sunshine

Feelings

Page 6
top:
1. annoyed
2. angry
3. sad
4. content

middle:
2. *e.g.* try, toy, top, tip
3. *e.g.* stile, stole, stone, shone

bottom:
1. tearful
2. happy
3. cross
4. well

Page 7
top:
2. tear
3. cross

Page 7 *(continued)*
middle:
Code is: how are you feeling today? write your answers in code!

Garden

Page 8
top:
1. fork (no e)
2. damson (no p)
3. lawn (no t)
4. flower (no t)
5. tulip (no s)

bottom:
1. greenhouse
2. hosepipe
3. lawnmower

Page 9
top:

```
G R A S S
    B U S H
F E R N
      F R U I T
W A L L
R O O T
    W E E D S
S E E D S
    R O S E S
```

The flower is a **sunflower**.

bottom:
2. thorn/prickle
3. stem/stalk
4. ruby/scarlet
5. perfume/scent

Sports

Page 10
top:
1. table-tennis, jogging, swimming, netball (all have double letters)
2. badminton, rounders, squash, hockey

bottom:
1. fencing, golf, hockey
2. badminton, curling, discus
3. cricket, high jump, trampolining
4. judo, karate, rowing

Page 11
top:
1. fastest
2. furthest
3. first
4. highest

bottom:

```
G O L F
L A C R O S S E
G Y M N A S T I C S
J U M P I N G
      P O L O
F E N C I N G
      C U R L I N G
      S W I M M I N G
```

The hidden word is **olympics**.

Snow

Page 12
top:
1. recipe (ends in 'ipe' not 'ice')
2. melting

middle:
1. skating
2. toboggan
3. snowman
4. icicles

bottom:
1. goose
2. chicken
3. bear
4. rabbit
5. cat

Page 13
top:
Code for summer is r t l l d q

1. shoes
2. flake
3. balls
4. man
5. drop
6. field
7. cap

Answers

Page 13 (continued)
1. snowballs
2. snowman
3. snowshoes
4. snowflake

Rescue
Page 14
top:
2. (banana, pear, grape) melon, peach, mango
3. (mouse, giraffe, lion) ox, monkey, zebra
4. (bus, coach, car) train, bicycle, lorry

bottom: *e.g.*
2. CAT   FAT   FAN   FIN
3. STOP   SHOP   CHOP   CHAP
4. SAFE   SALE   MALE   MOLE

Page 15
top:
1. higher 2. short 3. lowest 4. wider

middle:
2. fly 3. well 4. chest

bottom:

		F	L	A	M	E	S	
	P	A	N	I	C			
		R	E	S	C	U	E	
S	M	O	K	E				
		E	M	E	R	G	E	N	C	Y
N	I	N	E	N	I	N	E	N	I	N	E
	R	I	N	G				
	Q	U	I	C	K	L	Y	
S	I	R	E	N				
L	A	D	D	E	R			

The hidden word is **fire engine**.

Seaside
Page 16
top:
1. shells: limpets, mussels
2. food: sandwiches, apple, biscuits
3. drink: cola, squash, water
4. toys: frisbee, bat and ball
5. clothes: cap, bikini, T-shirt, sandals

Page 16 (continued)
bottom:
1. salt and pepper
2. Punch and Judy
3. bucket and spade
4. fish and chips

Page 17
top:
1. boulder and rock
2. ice and lolly
3. hat and cap

middle: *eg.*
1. seaside
2. sandcastle
3. afternoon
4. rockpool

bottom:
Code is; we have some chocolate to share, come along to the cave.

Castle
Page 18
top:
1. gong
2. slice
3. toe
4. title

bottom:
1. archers
2. arrow slits
3. bailey
4. battlements
5. gatehouse
6. horseman
7. keep
8. moat
9. portcullis
10. well

Page 19
top:
1. small
2. new
3. base
4. rich
5. full

Page 19 (continued)
bottom:

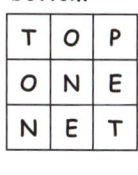

Picnic
Page 20
top:
1. ham (no e)
2. bananas (no p)
3. coca cola (no e)

middle:
1. ship
2. gauge
3. tell
4. maid

bottom:
sunny, park, football, swings, dog

Page 21
top:
1. glasses
2. bread
3. ham
4. cakes
5. grapes
6. pears
7. rolls

middle:
1. mea (t) una
2. mang (o) range
3. ha (m) elon
4. muffi (n) uts
5. chees (e) gg

bottom:

					P			
					E			
					C			
		C	A	S	H	E	W	
		N			A		A	
	P				Z		L	
	E				E		N	
B	R	A	Z	I	L		U	
	N						T	
	U							
	T							

31

Answers

Day Out
Page 22
top:
2. WHICH, POACH, CHIMP
3. PLEASE, PLENTY, SUPPLE
4. HOTEL, HOUSE, SHOP
5. CAMP, CANAL, PECAN

bottom:
2. flying, parking
3. return, repay
4. depart, delay

Page 23
top:
(HOT) cold
(SMALL) large
(WHITE) black
(SHORT) long
(LARGE) small
(WIDE-AWAKE) tired
(NO-ONE) everyone

bottom:
Code is: Shall we take mum to the fair or to the seaside?

Bugs
Page 24
top:
1. buy (has vowel u)
2. knee (is a four letter word)
3. kettle (no double e)
4. whisper (no a)

middle:
1. buzz
2. fly
3. slither
4. flap

bottom:
CAP, RAIN, BEE

Page 25
top:
1. flying, gliding
2. nip, bite
3. slide, slither
4. sing, chant

Page 25 (continued)
bottom:
1. mosquito (others end in e)
2. dragonfly (others include a double letter)
3. centipede (others start with s)
4. locust (others are one syllable and have a and n)

Treasure
Page 26
top:
1. lead (e)
2. stone (n)
3. money (y)

middle:
1. real
2. rent
3. lent
4. pint

bottom:
1. bangles
2. bracelets
3. clips
4. necklaces
5. rings
6. watches

Page 27
top:
2. fiddle
3. fresh
4. fork
5. fast

bottom:

Party Time
Page 28
top:
1. jelly (others are two words)
2. muffins (no a)
3. apple (is not a drink)

middle:
1. Jacky
2. Jacob
3. Callum
4. Lily
5. Joe
6. Ali
7. Meera
8. Thomas

bottom:
1. Abraham
2. Alex
3. Alison
4. Amanda
5. Angela
6. Anna
7. Annie
8. Antony

Page 29
top:
1. hat – cap
2. bowl – dish
3. frock – dress
4. streamers – paper chain

bottom:

B	O	O	K	S			
P	E	N	C	I	L	S	
F	O	O	T	B	A	L	L
C	A	M	E	R	A		

The mystery present is a **kite**.